AMISH
Butters, Salsas & Spreads

AMISH

Butters, Salsas & Spreads

Making and Canning Sweet and Savory Jams, Preserves, Conserves, and More

Laura Anne Lapp

Good Books

New York, New York

Good Books books may be purchased in bulk at special discounts for sales promotion, corporate gifts, fund-raising, or educational purposes. Special editions can also be created to specifications. For details, contact the Special Sales Department, Good Books, 307 West 36th Street, 11th Floor, New York, NY 10018 or info@skyhorsepublishing.com.

Good Books is an imprint of Skyhorse Publishing, Inc.®, a Delaware corporation.

Visit our website at www.goodbooks.com.

Library of Congress Cataloging-in-Publication Data is available on file.

Cover design by Daniel Brount
Cover image courtesy of Getty Images
Interior photos courtesy of Getty Images

Skyhorse ISBN: 978-1-68099-599-2
10 9 8 7 6 5 4 3 2

Ollies ISBN: 978-1-68099-809-2
10 9 8 7 6 5 4 3 2 1

Ebook ISBN: 978-1-68099-631-9

Printed in the United States of America

CONTENTS

INTRODUCTION

The recipes in this book are mostly "fun" recipes that aren't exactly staples in a pantry but definitely add flavor and excitement to many dishes. I like to have some recipes like this on hand for whenever I need a project. Even in wintertime, you can make a fresh batch of fruit spreads or preserves using canned fruits. Salsa is more of a warm-weather canning project, as you'll want to use fresh produce for the best flavor.

I hope you enjoy these recipes, and don't forget, homemade, canned foods make great gifts!

There are a few recipes in here that are not for canning, such as our traditional cheese and peanut butter spreads we serve at our church lunches. I hope you enjoy those as well.

Canning Tools and Equipment

Before you begin, there are a few items you will need to acquire if you haven't canned before. Most are fairly inexpensive and you can reuse them year after year.

Jars and Lids

I recommend buying new jars if you haven't canned before, because any small chips or cracks can keep the jar from obtaining a tight seal. New jars come complete with lids and rings (also called screw bands). Lids are usually used once, but rings can be reused.

Canner or Large Pot

I use the boiling-water method to process canned goods. That's the only way I can, since Amish families don't have electricity in their homes, but plenty of people use pressure canners. A boiling water canner is essentially a large pot that includes a canning rack. I often use my 12-quart stainless steel pot as a canner, especially when doing a small batch of something. Since I don't have a rack that fits in my pot, I usually put a clean dishcloth on the bottom before I put my jars in. It keeps them from clattering as they boil.

Jar Lifter

You will also need a jar lifter to remove the jars from the boiling water. They are inexpensive and oh so helpful!

Funnel

A funnel to get the food into the jars is also very useful, especially when canning jellies and salsas.

Canning Tips

- Heating your jars before filling them is important, not as a means of sterilizing them, but to reduce the stress of temperature change. I usually wash mine in hot water and allow them to air dry.
- When filling your jars, be sure to allow ½ inch of headspace (the space between the top of the food and the lid of the jar). Do not fill jars all the way to the top, because the jars won't seal as well, and also it can cause a sticky mess with sugary liquid escaping the jars.
- Be sure to wipe the rims of the jars well before placing the lids and tightening the rings. The rings don't have to be extremely tight—just use your fingers to tighten them as you would any jar you are closing.

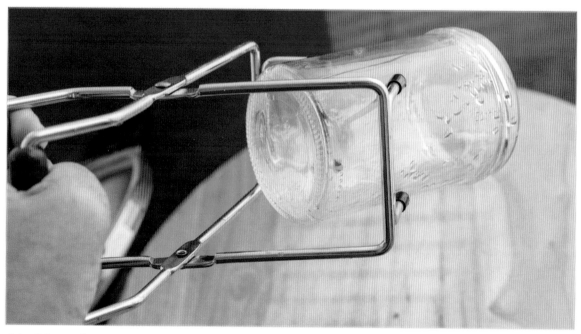

A jar lifter makes removing the jars from the boiling water much easier and safer.

- The jars should be covered with water after you place them in the canner. Allow the water to come to a full rolling boil before you start your timer to track the processing time indicated in the recipe.
- When the processing time is complete, remove jars from canner and allow to stand for 24 hours before moving them to your basement or pantry. Basement storage is ideal as the temperature is often cooler and better controlled.
- If your jars are sticky or have any residue on the outside, wipe them well before storing.
- Home-canned food is generally considered safe for one year. Any discoloration or strange smells are obviously not good and indicate that you should discard the food immediately.
- All canned food that is opened and not consumed must be refrigerated.

Note: The USDA suggests using water bath canning, as opposed to pressure canning, for preserving foods with high acid levels such as most tomatoes, relishes, jams, jellies, fruit butters, and marmalades.

The term pH is a measure of acidity; the lower its value, the more acidic the food. High acid foods (such as most of the ingredients in this cookbook) have a pH of 4.6 or lower. The one exception in this cookbook is tomatoes. Although tomatoes are usually considered a high acid food, some have pH values slightly above 4.6, therefore, in the process of preserving tomatoes, they must be acidified to a pH of 4.6 or lower with lemon juice, vinegar, or citric acid prior to processing. Thus, in this book you'll see vinegar or some kind of citrus juice added to recipes that include tomatoes.

Salsas

Salsa is one of my favorite things to can, especially when my sisters and I get together and spend the day helping each other. Chopping and dicing is so much more fun when done in the company of loved ones. There's a good collection of salsas in this section—not just traditional tomato salsas, but ones that feature a variety of vegetables, and even some fruits! So plan a "salsa day" with family or friends and get to it!

CORN RELISH (OR SALSA)

Yield: Approximately 6 pints

Ingredients:

2 quarts corn, cut from cobs
1 quart chopped cabbage
1 cup chopped red bell peppers
1 cup chopped green bell peppers
1 cup chopped onions
1 tablespoon celery seed
1 tablespoon salt
1 tablespoon turmeric
2 tablespoons dry mustard
1 tablespoon mustard seed
1 cup water
1 quart vinegar
2 cups sugar

Instructions:

1. In a large saucepan, combine all ingredients.

2. Bring to a boil, stirring occasionally.

3. Simmer for 20 minutes.

4. Ladle into clean jars.

5. Process in boiling-water bath for 10 minutes.

GREEN SALSA

Yield: Approximately 4 pints

Ingredients:

7 cups chopped, peeled green tomatoes

6–12 jalapeño peppers, chopped* (you may add or substitute your choice of hotter peppers if you wish)

2 cups chopped red onions

½ cup lime juice

½–¾ cup chopped cilantro

2 teaspoons ground cumin

1 teaspoon dried oregano

1 teaspoon salt

2 teaspoons ground black pepper

*Wear rubber gloves when chopping hot peppers to avoid skin irritation.

Instructions:

1. Combine all ingredients in a large saucepan.

2. Bring to a boil over medium heat.

3. Boil gently for 10–15 minutes, or until slightly thickened.

4. Ladle into clean jars.

5. Process in boiling-water bath for 10 minutes.

SALSA

Ingredients:
8 cups chopped, peeled tomatoes
2 cups chopped onion
1 cup chopped green peppers
8 jalapeño peppers, chopped*
3 cloves garlic, peeled and minced
1 (6-ounce) can tomato paste
¾ cup apple cider vinegar
¼–½ cup finely chopped cilantro
½ teaspoon ground cumin

*Wear rubber gloves when chopping hot peppers to avoid skin irritation.

Instructions:
1. Combine all ingredients in a large saucepan.

2. Bring to a boil, stirring constantly.

3. Reduce heat and simmer for 30 minutes, or until thickened.

4. Ladle hot salsa into clean jars.

5. Process for 20 minutes in boiling-water bath.

SUMMER SALSA

Yield: Approximately 4 pints

Ingredients:

7 cups chopped tomatoes
2 cups chopped cucumbers
2 cups chopped banana peppers
I cup chopped onion
½ cup chopped jalapeño peppers*
½ cup apple cider vinegar
¼ cup packed finely chopped cilantro
I tablespoon oregano
I teaspoon salt

*Wear rubber gloves when chopping hot peppers to avoid skin irritation.

Instructions:

1. Combine all ingredients in a medium saucepan.

2. Bring to a boil, stirring often.

3. Boil gently for 10–15 minutes, or until thickened.

4. Ladle into clean jars.

5. Process for 15 minutes in boiling-water bath.

CARROT SALSA

Yield: Approximately 4 pints

Ingredients:
6 cups chopped tomatoes
3 cups grated carrots
1½ cups apple cider vinegar
1¼ cups brown sugar
½ cup chopped onion
¼–½ cup chopped jalapeño peppers*
1½ teaspoon salt
½ teaspoon black pepper (or to taste)
¼ cup chopped cilantro (optional)

*Wear rubber gloves when chopping hot peppers to avoid skin irritation.

Instructions:
1. Combine all ingredients except cilantro (if using).

2. Bring to a boil over medium heat, stirring occasionally.

3. Boil gently until thickened, approximately 45 minutes.

4. Ladle into clean jars.

5. Process in boiling-water bath for 15 minutes.

Note: This salsa is almost a relish and is delicious served with meats or on crackers or chips.

PEACH SALSA

Yield: Approximately 4 pints

Ingredients:

6 cups peeled, chopped peaches
½ cup white vinegar
1¼ cups chopped onion
4 jalapeño peppers, chopped*
1 red bell pepper, chopped
½ cup finely chopped cilantro
1 clove garlic, finely chopped
1½ teaspoons cumin
½–1 teaspoon cayenne pepper (to taste)

*Wear rubber gloves when chopping hot peppers to avoid skin irritation.

Instructions:

1. Place chopped peaches into bowl with vinegar to prevent browning. Add remaining ingredients.

2. Bring to a boil over medium heat.

3. Boil gently until thickened, approximately 10–15 minutes.

4. Ladle into clean jars.

5. Process for 15 minutes in boiling-water bath.

PEAR SALSA

Yield: Approximately 4 pints

Ingredients:
1 cup vinegar
8 cups peeled, chopped pears
3 red bell peppers, chopped
3 green bell peppers, chopped
1 cup sugar
2 tablespoons salt
2 teaspoons ground mustard
1 teaspoon turmeric
½–1 teaspoon black pepper (to taste)

Instructions:
1. Combine vinegar and chopped pears to prevent browning.

2. Combine pears and vinegar with remaining ingredients in a medium saucepan.

3. Bring to a boil over medium heat.

4. Boil gently until thickened, approximately 10–15 minutes.

5. Ladle into clean jars.

6. Process for 20 minutes in boiling-water bath.

SANDWICH SPREAD

Yield: Approximately 7 pints

Ingredients:

6 large onions
6 green tomatoes
6 green bell peppers
6 red bell peppers
¼ cup salt
2 cups white vinegar
2 cups water
6 cups sugar
1 tablespoon prepared mustard
1 teaspoon turmeric

Instructions:

1. Finely chop or grind onions, tomatoes, and peppers.

2. Sprinkle with ¼ cup salt. Allow to rest for 3 hours.

3. Drain vegetable mixture well. Add vinegar and water to vegetables.

4. Bring to a boil and continue boiling for 15 minutes.

5. Add sugar, mustard, and turmeric.

6. Boil for 5 more minutes, stirring often.

7. Ladle into clean jars.

8. Process for 10 minutes in boiling-water bath.

Note: This spread is delicious mixed with mayonnaise!

SANDWICH SPREAD (VARIATION 2)

Yield: Approximately 7 pints

Ingredients:

6 onions
6 cucumbers
6 green bell peppers
12 green tomatoes
5 cups white sugar
3 tablespoons salt
2 cups vinegar
2 cups prepared mustard
1 tablespoon turmeric
2 tablespoons celery seed

Instructions:

1. Grind or chop vegetables, then drain in colander for 1 hour.

2. In a large saucepan, combine drained vegetables with sugar, salt, and vinegar.

3. Boil for 15 minutes.

4. Add remaining ingredients and boil for 5 more minutes.

5. Ladle into clean jars.

6. Process in boiling-water bath for 10 minutes.

CORN SALSA

Yield: Approximately 2 pints

Ingredients:

4 large fresh ears corn
1 cup chopped onion
1 cup chopped red or green bell peppers
1 cup chopped tomatoes
1 fresh jalapeño pepper, seeded and chopped*
½ cup lime juice
½–1 teaspoon salt (to taste)
½ teaspoon ground cumin
½–1 teaspoon black pepper (to taste)

*Wear rubber gloves when chopping hot peppers to avoid skin irritation.

Instructions:

1. Remove husks from corn, rinse, and cut kernels from cobs.

2. In a large saucepan, combine 2 cups corn kernels along with other ingredients.

3. Bring to a boil and simmer for 10 minutes.

4. Ladle into clean jars.

5. Process in boiling-water bath for 15 minutes.

Peanut Butter Spreads, Cheese Spreads, and Hand-Rolled Butter

There are two spreads that all Amish women make: peanut butter spread and the cheese spreads that are served at church for lunch. These are not spreads that we preserve; we make them fresh to serve right away, though they will keep for several weeks in the refrigerator. They are delicious on bread and toast.

PEANUT BUTTER SPREAD (VARIATION ONE)

Yield: Approximately 4 quarts

Ingredients:
⅔ cup Karo
9 cups brown sugar
4 cups water
5–6 pounds peanut butter
3 (1-quart) containers marshmallow crème

Instructions:
1. Heat Karo, brown sugar, and water until boiling.

2. Cool completely.

3. Stir cooled syrup into peanut butter

4. Stir in marshmallow crème.

Note: This spread is best served at room temperature.

PEANUT BUTTER SPREAD (VARIATION 2)

Yield: Approximately 3 quarts

Ingredients:

4 pounds peanut butter

2 pounds butter, room temperature

2 quarts Karo

1–2 quarts marshmallow crème

Instructions:

1. Cream together peanut butter and butter

2. Mix well and add remaining ingredients

Note: This version is not quite as sweet as some peanut butter spreads. It's best served at room temperature.

PEANUT BUTTER SPREAD (VARIATION 3)

Yield: Approximately 5 quarts

Ingredients:

Part 1:

6¼ cups brown sugar

5 cups granulated sugar

5 cups water

1⅔ cups molasses (or king syrup)

Part 2:

5 pounds peanut butter

1–2 quarts marshmallow crème

16 ounces cream cheese

Note: This spread is best served at room temperature.

Instructions:

1. Boil all part 1 ingredients for 3 minutes. Cool the resulting syrup completely.

2. Combine part 2 ingredients and add cooled syrup, mixing until well combined.

PEANUT BUTTER SPREAD (VARIATION 4)

Yield: Approximately 3 quarts

Ingredients:

2 cups brown sugar

1 cup water

2 tablespoons light corn syrup

1 teaspoon maple flavoring

18 ounces peanut butter

7 ounces marshmallow crème

Instructions:

1. In a medium saucepan, combine brown sugar, water, corn syrup, and maple flavoring. Bring to a boil.

2. Cool the resulting syrup completely.

3. Add peanut butter to cooled syrup and mix thoroughly.

4. Add marshmallow crème and mix until blended.

Note: Best when served at room temperature.

CHEESE SPREAD (VARIATION 1)

Yield: Approximately 2 quarts

Ingredients:

2⅔ cups milk
8 tablespoons butter
½ teaspoon salt
40 slices American cheese

Instructions:

1. Heat milk and butter, stirring, just until boiling. Remove from heat.

2. Add salt.

3. Add cheese 1 slice at a time, stirring until dissolved.

4. Cool before serving.

Note: Best when served at room temperature.

CHEESE SPREAD (VARIATION 2)

Yield: Approximately 3 quarts

Ingredients:

8 cups milk
5 pounds American cheese
1 pound Velveeta, sliced or cubed

Instructions:

1. Heat milk until almost boiling.

2. Add cheeses 1 slice or cube at a time, stirring often.

3. Mix thoroughly.

4. Cool completely before serving.

Note: Best served at room temperature.

CHEESE SPREAD (VARIATION 3)

Yield: Approximately 4 quarts

Ingredients

3½ cups water

4 cups milk

2½ teaspoons baking soda

5 pounds American cheese slices

Instructions:

1. Heat water and milk until boiling.

2. Stir in baking soda and cheese, one slice at a time, stirring until melted and smooth.

3. Cool completely before serving.

Note: Best served at room temperature.

HAND-ROLLED BUTTER

Ingredients:

Cream

Salt

Note: Amish butter is known for its rich, creamy flavor, which is largely thanks to how the cows are raised. If you can't get cream straight from an Amish dairy farm, try to find a source where the cows are pasture raised, meaning they're at least mostly grass-fed and are free to move around outside their stalls. Fresh cream from a good source will make the difference in your butter's flavor.

Jar churns allow you to slowly churn the butter by cranking the handle manually for about twenty minutes. Another method is to put a marble in a mason jar and shake the jar until the cream separates into butter (just be careful not to shake so hard that the marble breaks the jar).

Instructions:

1. Thoroughly clean the inside of your butter churn with soap and hot water.

2. Pour cream into the churn, being sure not to fill the churn more than ⅔ full.

3. Crank briskly until the cream separates into buttermilk and butter. It will likely take about 20 minutes, but may take longer if you're making a bigger batch.

4. Pour off the buttermilk, reserving it for baking.

5. Dump butter into a bowl and pour cold fresh water over it. Use a wooden spoon to stir the butter in the water. Drain off the water and repeat. The goal is to remove as much of the buttermilk as possible so that only the actual butter remains.

6. Add salt to taste.

7. Place a sheet of parchment paper on a counter or other hard surface. Scoop the butter onto the paper in an oblong shape. Fold the paper over the butter and then use the edge of a cookie sheet or another long straight item to gently push the butter into a neat log shape.

8. Twist or tape the ends of the parchment paper to close. Store in the refrigerator.

Fruit Butters

Making fruit butters is fun and easy and there are lots of options to choose from. Fruit butter can be spread on bread or toast, of course, or used as a filling in layer cakes or cookies.

Fruit butters are simply fruit and sugar cooked over medium heat until thickened. Cooking times will vary from 30–60 minutes or more, depending on what kind of fruit is used, the ripeness of the fruit, and also the cooking temperature.

Cook the fruit butter until it thickens and begins to hold its shape on a spoon. When it's a nice spreading consistency, it's ready to spoon into jars for processing.

A note on fruit butters: All fruit must be cooked until soft, then put through a food mill or a food processor until a nice, even texture is acquired. Fruit butters can be stored in the refrigerator for several weeks if canning isn't something you enjoy or have time for.

APPLE CIDER BUTTER

Yield: Approximately 4 pints

Ingredients:

6 pounds apples, peeled, cored, and quartered

2 cups apple cider

3 cups sugar

1½ teaspoons cinnamon (or to taste)

Instructions:

1. Combine apples and cider in a medium pot and boil gently until apples are soft.

2. Carefully ladle hot apples into food mill and process.

3. Add 12 cups of puree and the remaining ingredients to a medium stainless steel or heavy kettle. (If you have additional puree, enjoy as applesauce!)

4. Bring to a boil over medium heat, reduce heat, and stir often, especially when butter begins to thicken.

5. When butter is thick and spreadable, ladle into clean jars and process for 10 minutes in boiling-water bath.

APRICOT BUTTER

Yield: Approximately 4 pints

Ingredients:

2 pounds apricots, peeled and pitted

½ cup water

3 cups sugar

2 tablespoons lemon juice

Instructions:

1. Combine apricots and water in a medium pot and boil until apricots are soft.

2. Puree the softened fruit, using a food mill or food processor.

3. In a large pot, combine remaining ingredients with 6 cups of fruit puree (if you have additional puree, it makes good baby food or can be frozen for later use).

4. Bring to a boil over medium heat. Reduce heat and continue gently boiling, stirring often, until butter is thickened and spreadable.

5. Ladle hot butter into clean jars and process for 10 minutes in a boiling-water bath.

PEAR BUTTER

Ingredients:

3 quarts pears, peeled and cored

1 quart sugar

Instructions:

1. Boil pears until soft.

2. Drain well.

3. Mash pears with potato masher.

4. Stir in sugar and bring to a boil over medium heat.

5. Boil until thickened, stirring often.

6. Ladle into clean jars and process for 10 minutes in boiling-water bath.

GRAPE BUTTER

Yield: Approximately 4 pints

Ingredients:

1 quart grapes

1 quart sugar

Instructions:

1. Combine grapes and sugar in a medium saucepan.

2. Bring to a boil over medium heat. Reduce heat and boil gently for 20–25 minutes.

3. Strain and pour into clean jars.

4. Process for 10 minutes in boiling-water bath.

Note: This is an old-fashioned recipe. Concord grapes work great for this butter, but other dark grapes work fine too.

"MOCK" APPLE BUTTER

Yield: Approximately 6 pints

Ingredients:

2 quarts sweetened applesauce
2 cups brown sugar
1 cup white vinegar
1 tablespoon cinnamon
½ teaspoon cloves

Instructions:

1. Combine all ingredients in a large kettle

2. Bring to a boil over medium heat.

3. Reduce heat and simmer for 2 hours.

4. Ladle into clean jars and process for 10 minutes in boiling-water bath.

PEACH BUTTER

Yield: Approximately 4 pints

Ingredients:

4½ pounds peaches, peeled, pitted, and roughly chopped

½ cup water

2 tablespoons lemon juice

4 cups sugar

Instructions:

1. Combine peaches, water, and lemon juice in a medium pot. Boil until soft.

2. Process in food mill or food processor until smooth.

3. Stir peach puree and sugar to combine, then bring to a boil over medium heat.

4. Boil gently, stirring often, until thickened and spreadable.

5. Ladle into clean jars and process for 10 minutes in boiling-water bath.

PEPPER BUTTER

Yield: Approximately 7 pints

Ingredients:

42 yellow banana peppers
2 cups chopped onions
1½ cups white vinegar
2 cups prepared mustard
6½ cups sugar
1 tablespoon salt
1 cup Clear Jel (or THERMFLO)
1½ cups water

Instructions:

1. In a large pan, combine peppers, onions, vinegar, mustard, sugar, and salt.

2. Bring to a boil over medium heat and boil until peppers and onions are soft.

3. Dissolve Clear Jel in water. Stir into boiling pepper mixture.

4. Continue boiling for 2 minutes.

5. Ladle into clean jars and process for 10 minutes in boiling-water bath.

Note: This butter has the addition of Clear Jel, as there is no natural pectin in peppers.

PEAR BUTTER WITH PINEAPPLE

Yield: Approximately 4 pints

Ingredients:
12–14 medium pears, peeled and cored
8 cups sugar
1 (20-ounce) can crushed pineapple
3 tablespoons lemon juice

Instructions:
1. Place pears in a medium pan and cook over medium heat until soft.

2. Process in food mill or food processor.

3. In the medium pan, combine pear puree with sugar, pineapple, and lemon juice.

4. Boil over medium heat, stirring often, until thickened and spreadable.

5. Ladle into clean jars and process for 20 minutes in boiling-water bath.

CRAN-APPLE BUTTER

Yield: Approximately 4 pints

Ingredients:

6 pounds apples, peeled and chopped
8 cups cranberry juice
4 cups sugar
1 tablespoon cinnamon (optional)
½ teaspoon nutmeg (optional)

Instructions:

1. In a large kettle, combine apples and cranberry juice.

2. Bring to a boil over medium heat and cook until soft.

3. Process apples in food mill or food processor until you have a smooth puree.

4. Back in the kettle, combine puree, sugar, and spices. Bring to a boil over medium heat and boil gently, stirring often, until mixture is thickened and spreadable.

5. Ladle into clean jars and process for 10 minutes in boiling-water bath.

BLUEBERRY BUTTER

Yield: Approximately 4 pints

Ingredients:

12 cups blueberries

3 cups water

3 cups sugar

2 tablespoons lemon juice

Instructions:

1. In a medium kettle, combine blueberries and water. Bring to a boil and mash berries slightly with potato masher. Continue boiling 5 minutes.

2. Drain well and puree in food mill or food processor.

3. Back in the kettle, combine berries, sugar, and lemon juice.

4. Bring to a boil over medium heat. Reduce heat and boil gently, stirring often, until thickened and spreadable.

5. Ladle into clean jars and process for 10 minutes in boiling-water bath.

CRANBERRY TANGERINE SPREAD

Yield: Approximately 3 pints

Ingredients:

1 (12-ounce) package cranberries
1 cup water
½ cup tangerine or orange juice
3 cups sugar
1–2 teaspoons cinnamon

Instructions:

1. In a kettle or saucepan, combine cranberries, water, and juice.

2. Boil until berries pop, then cool for 1 hour.

3. Blend berry mixture until smooth.

4. Back in the kettle or saucepan, combine sugar and cinnamon with berry mixture.

5. Bring to a boil, stirring constantly.

6. Simmer until thickened, stirring often.

7. Ladle into clean jars.

8. Process for 10 minutes in boiling-water bath.

MANGO-CITRUS SPREAD

Yield: Approximately 4 half-pints

Ingredients:

7 cups peeled and chopped mangoes
1 cup orange juice
¾ cup water
2½ cups sugar
2 tablespoons lemon or lime juice

Instructions:

1. Combine mangoes, orange juice, and water in a medium saucepan.

2. Simmer for approximately 30 minutes, stirring occasionally, until mangoes are very tender.

3. Puree mango mixture in food mill or food processor.

4. Return mango mixture to medium pan and add sugar and juice.

5. Bring to a boil over medium heat and simmer for approximately 35 minutes, or until thickened.

6. Ladle into clean jars and process for 10 minutes in boiling-water bath.

BROWN SUGAR–VANILLA BANANA BUTTER

Yield: Approximately 4 pints

Ingredients:

4 cups mashed bananas (approximately 12 very ripe bananas)

½ cup lemon juice

1 (1.75-ounce) box powdered fruit pectin.

½ teaspoon butter

2 teaspoons vanilla extract

4 cups brown sugar

2 cups sugar

Instructions:

1. In a large kettle or saucepan, combine mashed bananas, lemon juice, pectin, butter, and vanilla.

2. Bring to a boil over medium heat, stirring constantly.

3. Add sugars and boil hard for 1 minute, stirring constantly.

4. Ladle into clean jars and process for 10 minutes in boiling-water bath.

PEACH-HONEY BUTTER

Yield: Approximately 2 pints

Ingredients:

18 medium ripe peaches, peeled, pitted, and chopped

¼ cup water

2½ cups sugar

¾ cup honey

Instructions:

1. In a medium saucepan, combine peaches and water.

2. Simmer until peaches are tender, 10–15 minutes.

3. Puree peaches in a food mill or food processor until smooth.

4. Return puree to saucepan and add sugar and honey.

5. Simmer, stirring often, until mixture is thickened.

6. Ladle into clean jars and process for 10 minutes in boiling-water bath.

SPICED PUMPKIN BUTTER

Yield: Approximately 2 pints

Ingredients:

3½ cups cooked pumpkin or 2 (15-ounce) cans
   pumpkin puree
1¼ cups maple syrup
½ cup apple juice
2 tablespoons lemon juice
1 teaspoon ground cinnamon
½ teaspoon nutmeg

Instructions:

1. In a medium saucepan, combine all
   ingredients.

2. Bring to a boil, stirring often. Simmer until
   thickened, approximately 25 minutes.

3. Ladle into clean jars and process for
   10 minutes in boiling-water bath.

Jellies, Jams, and Preserves

This section includes both sweet and savory jellies, jams, and preserves that are made in a variety of ways—some use liquid pectin, some powdered pectin, and some Jell-O! Fruit pectin is found in most grocery stores in the summer, but Amish bulk food grocery stores usually stock it year-round, and I'm sure it would be available online as well.

JALAPEÑO JELLY

Yield: Approximately 2 pints

Ingredients:
2 cups chopped jalapeño peppers
2 cups apple cider vinegar
6 cups white sugar
2 (3-ounce) pouches liquid pectin

Instructions:
1. In a medium saucepan or kettle, combine peppers, vinegar, and sugar.

2. Bring to a boil, stirring often.

3. Stir in pectin. Bring to a boil again and boil hard for 1 minute.

4. Ladle into clean jars and process for 10 minutes in boiling-water bath.

CIDER JELLY

Yield: Approximately 2 pints

Ingredients:

4 cups apple cider
⅔ cups Red Hots (cinnamon candy)
1 (1.75-ounce) box powdered fruit pectin
5 cups sugar

Instructions:

1. In a medium saucepan, combine cider, Red Hots, and pectin and heat until pectin is dissolved.

2. Bring to a boil and add sugar. Boil vigorously (rolling boil) for 1 minute.

3. Ladle into clean jars and process for 10 minutes in boiling-water bath.

ELDERBERRY PRESERVES

Yield: Approximately 4 pints

Ingredients:

½ gallon Karo
½ gallon white sugar
1 pint elderberry juice

Instructions:

1. Combine all ingredients in a large saucepan.

2. Bring to a boil and continue boiling for 10 minutes.

3. Ladle into clean jars and process for 10 minutes in boiling-water bath.

RHUBARB JELLY

Yield: Approximately 4 pints

Ingredients:

5 cups chopped rhubarb

½ cup water

4–5 cups sugar

1 (6-ounce) package Jell-O, strawberry
or raspberry flavor

Instructions:

1. In a large saucepan, combine rhubarb,
   water, and sugar.

2. Bring to a boil over medium heat and boil
   for 5 minutes.

3. Remove from heat and stir in Jell-O.

4. Ladle into clean jars and process for
   10 minutes in boiling-water bath.

POMEGRANATE JELLY

Yield: Approximately 2 pints

Ingredients:

4 cups pomegranate juice
¼ cup lemon juice
1 (1.75-ounce) package powdered fruit pectin
4½–5 cups sugar

Instructions:

1. In a medium saucepan, combine pomegranate juice and lemon juice.

2. Sprinkle pectin over juice and stir to dissolve.

3. Bring to a boil, stirring often.

4. Add sugar.

5. Return to a boil and boil hard for 1 minute.

6. Ladle jelly into clean jars and process for 10 minutes in boiling-water bath.

ZUCCHINI JAM

Yield: Approximately 4 pints

Ingredients:

6 cups peeled, seeded, and chopped or grated
   zucchini (if the zucchini are shorter than 6 inches,
   you may not need to seed them)
6 cups sugar
6 tablespoons lemon juice
6 tablespoons orange or lemon Jell-O

Instructions:

1. In a medium saucepan, combine zucchini and sugar.

2. Bring to a boil and continue boiling for 6–8 minutes.

3. Stir in lemon juice and Jell-O. Boil for 6 more minutes.

4. Ladle into clean jars and process for 10 minutes in boiling-water bath.

ROSEMARY-PEAR PRESERVES

Yield: Approximately 3 pints

Ingredients:

4–6 pounds firm ripe pears, such as Bartlett
3 cups sugar
1 cup honey
½ cup lemon juice
1–2 teaspoons fresh rosemary

Instructions:

1. Peel, core, and finely chop pears.

2. Measure 8 cups pears into medium saucepan. Add sugar, honey, and lemon juice.

3. Bring to a boil, stirring often.

4. Stir in rosemary and simmer for 20–25 minutes until mixture is slightly thickened.

5. Ladle into clean jars and process for 10 minutes in boiling-water bath.

PEPPERED-PLUM JAM

Yield: Approximately 2 pints

Ingredients:

4 pounds plums

½ cup water

8 cups sugar

1 (1.75-ounce) package powdered fruit pectin

1–2 teaspoons ground black pepper

Instructions:

1. Peel, pit, and chop plums. Combine plums and water in medium saucepan.

2. Bring to a boil and simmer for 5 minutes.

3. Measure 6 cups cooked plums and return to saucepan. Any excess plums can be pureed and used for baby food, eaten with yogurt, or frozen for later use.

4. Add sugar to plums and bring to a boil, stirring constantly.

5. Stir in pectin.

6. Return to full boil and boil hard for 1 minute.

7. Remove from heat and stir in pepper.

8. Ladle into clean jars and process for 10 minutes in boiling-water bath.

ZUCCHINI JELLY WITH PINEAPPLE

Yield: Approximately 4 pints

Ingredients:

6 cups grated zucchini

6 cups sugar

½ cup lemon juice

I cup crushed pineapple

I (6-ounce) package Jell-O (flavor of your choice)

Instructions:

1. In a medium saucepan, bring zucchini to a boil.

2. Continue boiling for 20 minutes.

3. Add sugar and boil for 6 minutes.

4. Add lemon juice, pineapple, and Jell-O.

5. Boil for 10 more minutes.

6. Ladle into clean jars and process for 10 minutes in boiling-water bath.

CARROT CAKE JAM

Yield: Approximately 4 pints

Ingredients:

2 cups finely shredded carrots
1 cup peeled chopped pears
1 (15-ounce) can crushed pineapple, undrained
2 tablespoons lemon juice
1 teaspoon cinnamon
1 (1.75-ounce box) powdered fruit pectin
4 cups sugar
2 cups brown sugar
1 teaspoon vanilla

Instructions:

1. In a medium-size heavy saucepan, combine carrots, pears, pineapple, lemon juice, and cinnamon.

2. Bring to a boil over medium heat. Simmer for 20 minutes, stirring often.

3. Remove from heat. Sprinkle pectin over mixture and stir until dissolved.

4. Bring mixture to a boil, stirring constantly.

5. Add sugar.

6. Bring to a full boil and boil hard for 1 minute.

7. Remove from heat and stir in vanilla.

8. Ladle into clean jars and process for 10 minutes in boiling-water bath.

TOMATO BASIL JAM

Yield: Approximately 2 pints

Ingredients:

2½ pounds ripe tomatoes, peeled
¼ cup lemon juice
3 tablespoons fresh, chopped basil
1 (1.75-ounce) box powdered fruit pectin
3 cups sugar

Instructions:

1. Chop tomatoes into small pieces.

2. Measure 3½ cups tomatoes into medium saucepan.

3. Bring to a boil, stirring often.

4. Simmer tomatoes for 10 minutes, stirring often.

5. Stir in lemon juice and basil.

6. Stir in pectin and bring to a full rolling boil, stirring constantly.

7. Add sugar and return to boil.

8. Boil hard for 1 minute.

9. Ladle into clean jars and process for 10 minutes in boiling-water bath.

BLACKBERRY JAM

Yield: Approximately 2 cups

Ingredients:

3 cups blackberries

⅓ cup sugar

¼ cup molasses

¼ cup + 3 tablespoons orange juice, divided

3 tablespoons cornstarch

Instructions:

1. In a medium heavy saucepan, combine blackberries, sugar, molasses, and 3 tablespoons orange juice.

2. Simmer for 5 minutes, uncovered, stirring often.

3. Combine remaining ¼ cup orange juice with cornstarch. Stir into blackberry mixture.

4. Cook and stir until thickened.

5. Cool, then store in refrigerator for up to 2 weeks.

Note: This a "fresh" jam that can be used immediately or stored in the refrigerator.

RASPBERRY JAM

Yield: Approximately 4 pints

Ingredients:

8 cups raspberries

1 (1.75-ounce box) powdered fruit pectin

7 cups sugar

Instructions:

1. Mash berries, using a potato masher, until fairly smooth.

2. Measure out 5 cups berries.

3. Pour into a medium-size heavy saucepan.

4. Stir in pectin and bring to a full rolling boil, stirring constantly.

5. Add sugar and return to boil, stirring constantly.

6. Boil hard for 1 minute.

7. Ladle into clean jars and process for 10 minutes in boiling-water bath.

STRAWBERRY JAM

Yield: Approximately 5 pints

Ingredients:

12 cups strawberries

1 (1.75-ounce) box fruit pectin

½–1 teaspoon butter (optional)

7 cups sugar

Instructions:

1. Using a potato masher, mash berries until fairly smooth.

2. Measure 5 cups berries into a medium-size heavy saucepan.

3. Stir in pectin and butter, if using.

4. Bring to a full boil, stirring constantly.

5. Add sugar and return to boil, stirring constantly.

6. Boil hard for 1 minute.

7. Ladle jam into clean jars and process for 10 minutes in boiling-water bath.

RED PEPPER-GARLIC JELLY

Yield: Approximately 2 pints

Ingredients:

1½ cups finely chopped red bell peppers

3 garlic cloves (large), finely chopped

¾ cup apple cider vinegar

3 cups white sugar

1 (3-ounce) pouch liquid pectin

Instructions:

1. In a large saucepan, combine peppers, garlic, vinegar, and sugar.

2. Bring to a full rolling boil, stirring often.

3. Add pectin and bring to a full boil. Boil hard for 1 minute. Remove from heat.

4. Ladle into clean jars and process for 10 minutes in boiling-water bath.

Note: These savory jellies call for liquid pectin, sold in bags or pouches. They are available wherever canning supplies are sold.

BASIL PEPPER JAM

Yield: Approximately 2 pints

Ingredients:

½–1 cup chopped banana peppers

¼–½ cup chopped red or green chile peppers (or your choice of hot peppers)

½ cup chopped red onion

4 large basil leaves, thinly sliced

½ teaspoon dried basil

¾ cup white vinegar

3 cups white sugar

1 (3-ounce) pouch liquid pectin

Instructions:

1. In a large saucepan, combine all ingredients except liquid pectin.

2. Bring to a boil over high heat, stirring often.

3. While boiling, add pectin, stirring often. Boil hard for 1 minute.

4. Ladle into clean jars and process for 10 minutes in boiling-water bath.

RED ONION JELLY

Yield: Approximately 2 pints

Ingredients:

1½ cups finely chopped red onion
2 teaspoons lemon zest
¾ cup white vinegar
3 cups white sugar
1 (3-ounce) liquid pectin

Instructions:

1. In a large saucepan, combine all ingredients except pectin.

2. Bring to a full rolling boil, stirring often.

3. Stir in pectin and boil hard for 1 minute, stirring constantly.

4. Ladle into clean jars and process for 10 minutes in boiling-water bath.

Fruit Conserves

Fruit conserves are a mix of fresh fruit, dried fruit, nuts, and spices. They are a welcome change from regular jellies and jams and can be used in many ways—as spreads on toast or muffins, as an accompaniment to cheese, or even as a dessert topping.

Note: A gel test is a handy way to see if your conserves are done and ready to process. To test, dip a cold metal spoon into your boiling mixture. If the drops are light and syrupy and drip off the spoon one by one, it's not done. Continue checking until mixture falls from spoon in a sheet.

SOUR CHERRY CONSERVE

Yield: Approximately 4 pints

Ingredients:

3 oranges, peeled and seeds removed
3 lemons, peeled and seeds removed
5 cups sour cherries
2 cups chopped apples
½ cup water
4 cups sugar
¾ cup walnuts

Instructions:

1. Chop oranges and lemons into pulp. Place in large kettle or saucepan.

2. Add cherries, apples, and water.

3. Bring to a boil over medium heat, stirring often. Continue boiling for 10 minutes, or until cherries are softened.

4. Add sugar and continue boiling for 30 minutes or until thickened. Add nuts and boil for 5 minutes longer.

5. Ladle into clean jars and process for 10 minutes in boiling-water bath.

PLUM CONSERVE

Yield: Approximately 4 pints

Ingredients:

5 pounds plums, peeled, halved, and pitted
6½ cups sugar
4 cups raisins or dried cranberries
2 tablespoons orange zest
1 cup orange juice
2 cups walnuts, chopped

Instructions:

1. In a large saucepan, combine all ingredients except nuts.

2. Bring to a boil over medium heat, stirring often.

3. Continue boiling for 40 minutes, or until thickened.

4. Add nuts and boil for 5 minutes.

5. Ladle into clean jars and process for 10 minutes in boiling-water bath.

GOOSEBERRY CONSERVE

Yield: Approximately 3 pints

Ingredients:

6 cups gooseberries, stemmed
1 cup raisins or dried cranberries
¾–1 cup peeled, seeded, and chopped oranges
4½ cups sugar

Instructions:

1. In a medium saucepan, combine all ingredients.

2. Bring to a boil over medium heat, stirring often.

3. Continue boiling gently, stirring often, for 35 minutes, or until thickened.

4. Ladle into clean jars and process for 10 minutes in boiling-water bath.

CHERRY CONSERVES

Yield: Approximately 3 pints

Ingredients:

6 cups sour or sweet cherries
1 cup dried cranberries
1 cup seeded, chopped oranges
4 cups sugar

Instructions:

1. In a medium saucepan, combine all ingredients.

2. Bring to a boil over medium heat.

3. Continue boiling for 30 minutes or until thickened.

4. Ladle into clean jars and process for 10 minutes in boiling-water bath.

APRICOT ORANGE CONSERVE

Yield: Approximately 3 pints

Ingredients:

4 cups pitted, peeled, chopped apricots

2 tablespoons orange zest

1½ cups orange juice

2 tablespoons lemon juice

4 cups sugar

½ cup chopped walnuts or pecans.

Instructions:

1. In a large saucepan, combine all ingredients except nuts.

2. Bring to a boil over medium heat, stirring often, and boil hard for 15–20 minutes, or until thickened.

3. Add nuts and boil for 5 minutes more.

4. Ladle into clean jars and process for 10 minutes in boiling-water bath.

CRANBERRY CONSERVE

Yield: Approximately 3 pints

Ingredients:

1 orange, peeled, seeded, and finely chopped
1½ cups water
4 cups cranberries
½ cup raisins
3 cups sugar
½ cup walnuts or pecans

Instructions:

1. In a large saucepan, combine orange and water and boil for 5 minutes.

2. Add cranberries, raisins, and sugar and bring to a boil, stirring often.

3. Continue boiling approximately 20 minutes, or until thickened.

4. Add nuts and continue boiling for 5 minutes, stirring constantly.

5. Ladle into clean jars and process for 10 minutes in boiling-water bath.

APPLE CONSERVE

Yield: Approximately 3 pints

Ingredients:

4 cups unsweetened applesauce
2½ cups pineapple crushed, drained
½ cup chopped, dried apples
¾–1 cup golden raisins
1½ tablespoons lemon juice
1 teaspoons ground cinnamon

Instructions:

1. In a large saucepan, combine all ingredients.

2. Bring to a boil over medium heat, stirring often.

3. Continue boiling for 20 minutes or until thickened.

4. Ladle in clean jars and process for 10 minutes in boiling-water bath.

AMBROSIA CONSERVE

Yield: Approximately 3 pints

Ingredients:

6 cups chopped fresh pineapple

Zest and juice from 2 oranges

6 cups sugar

1 cup coconut, flaked

1 cup chopped, drained maraschino cherries

Instructions:

1. In a large saucepan, combine pineapple with orange juice and zest.

2. Boil for 10 minutes, or until pineapple is soft.

3. Add sugar and boil hard for 15 minutes, stirring often.

4. Add coconut and cherries. Boil for 5 more minutes.

5. Ladle into clean jars and process for 10 minutes in boiling-water bath.

CONVERSION CHARTS

METRIC AND IMPERIAL CONVERSIONS
(These conversions are rounded for convenience)

Ingredient	Cups/Tablespoons/Teaspoons	Ounces	Grams/Milliliters
Butter	1 cup/ 16 tablespoons/ 2 sticks	8 ounces	230 grams
Cheese, shredded	1 cup	4 ounces	110 grams
Cream cheese	1 tablespoon	0.5 ounce	14.5 grams
Cornstarch	1 tablespoon	0.3 ounce	8 grams
Flour, all-purpose	1 cup/1 tablespoon	4.5 ounces/0.3 ounce	125 grams/8 grams
Flour, whole wheat	1 cup	4 ounces	120 grams
Fruit, dried	1 cup	4 ounces	120 grams
Fruits or veggies, chopped	1 cup	5 to 7 ounces	145 to 200 grams
Fruits or veggies, pureed	1 cup	8.5 ounces	245 grams
Honey, maple syrup, or corn syrup	1 tablespoon	0.75 ounce	20 grams
Liquids: cream, milk, water, or juice	1 cup	8 fluid ounces	240 milliliters
Oats	1 cup	5.5 ounces	150 grams
Salt	1 teaspoon	0.2 ounce	6 grams
Spices: cinnamon, cloves, ginger, or nutmeg (ground)	1 teaspoon	0.2 ounce	5 milliliters
Sugar, brown, firmly packed	1 cup	7 ounces	200 grams
Sugar, white	1 cup/1 tablespoon	7 ounces/0.5 ounce	200 grams/12.5 grams
Vanilla extract	1 teaspoon	0.2 ounce	4 grams

OVEN TEMPERATURES

Fahrenheit	Celsius	Gas Mark
225°	110°	¼
250°	120°	½
275°	140°	1
300°	150°	2
325°	160°	3
350°	180°	4
375°	190°	5
400°	200°	6
425°	220°	7
450°	230°	8

INDEX

AMISH

Canning & Preserving

How to Make Soups, Sauces, Pickles, Relishes, and More

Laura Anne Lapp

60 Simple, Classic Recipes

NOTES

NOTES

NOTES

NOTES

NOTES

NOTES

NOTES

NOTES

NOTES

NOTES

NOTES

NOTES

NOTES

NOTES

NOTES